The **Strange I of Marple**

and the family who lived there

Steve Cliffe, illustrated by David Kelsall

Should you ask me whence these stories, whence these legends and traditions? I should tell you, I repeat them as I heard them, in the vale of the green valley, by the pleasant water courses – Longfellow

Acknowledgements

Thanks to Mark Whittaker of Marple Website (www.marple.website) , The Virtual History Tour of Marple (https://visit marple.co.uk) and Marple Local History Society (www.mlhs.org.uk). For further reading about Marple Hall visit (www.marple.website/marplehall) Modern photos and illustrations are by David Kelsall or Steve Cliffe.

Published by SH Publications 2019 Mini Series

ISBN 978-0-9514611-4-3

SH Publications

Prologue

The small child lay breathless in bed as the floorboards creaked in the old wooden panelled bedroom. Richard did not like the way the hinges squealed on the dark oak door when it opened. And although he was used to the shadows cast by a small night light at his bedside, what terrified him was that the door had NOT opened… yet SOMETHING was in the room. And that something was making a distinct thump, thump, thump on the floorboards as it approached his cot.

Entrance hall with suits of armour

Marple Hall and stables

Marple Hall

"It was a great house, but full of wickedness… no wonder the spirits of its former inhabitants cannot find rest"

So said a former tenant of the old hall, which once stood darkly festooned with

3

ivy and shrouded by trees on a steep slope towering above the River Goyt, whose murky waters still glide sinuously through Marple Dale on their journey into urban, busy Stockport town.

All that remains of former glory at Marple Hall are a few old stones marking the foundations, but giving little idea of the extant of the great house and its stables with clock tower, the great barn and rolling parkland, where generations of Bradshaws and Isherwoods pursued the leisured life of country gentry enjoying their status as "Squires" of Marple, riding out in their antiquated horse drawn carriages, and receiving the bows, nods and doffed caps of local people. At Marple church they had their own coach house with a stone cut coat of arms, and their own curtained pew with fireplace, where they could listen to the service comfortably in easy chairs as servants stoked the fire.

They were not always so grand – being descendants of tillers of the land and journeymen craftspeople. In 1606 the Bradshaws were tenant farmers at Marple Hall and Wyberslegh Hall farm in High Lane, but prosperous enough to buy both. These two medieval hall houses were then partially rebuilt and extended by the Bradshaws, so that the formerly black and white timbered farmhouses which would have been recognised by old lords of the manor, the medieval de Vernons and Stanley families, were instead clad in the russet grey stone of the neighbourhood.

Marple and Wyberslegh manors originally belonged to the Earls of Chester but were given late in the 1100s to Robert, baron of Stockport in return for his services as a Forester of Fee whose duties were to look after "vert or venison" in the Earl's hunting forest of Macclesfield, which then extended as far north as Otterspool Bridge, and was bounded to the east by the River Goyt. Vert and venison referred to the trees (vert = greenery) and venison, now deer meat, covered all animals of the chase – deer, hare, wild boar, wild cattle, wolves and bears. Of all these animals roaming the forest, only hares and deer remain. The wild cattle of Lyme Park died out in the 19th century, wolves bears and wild boar were hunted to extinction long before.

Judge John Bradshawe

The early manor house of the Vernons, who received the manor from Robert de Stokeport as a dowry in the 1220s after William de Vernon married his sister Margery, was Old Manor

Farm, still standing and hidden in the trees above Dan Bank. It boasts a cruck framed medieval hall open to the roof. Later on a Richard de Vernon was given rights by the Earl of Chester to clear land in the forest at Marple and Wyberslegh. Either they or the Stanleys built Wyberslegh Hall in High Lane and cleared the surrounding forest land. The circular pattern of the fields surrounding this house can still be made out.

When the Bradshaws bought Marple Hall in the 17th century it was not known to be haunted, though the story of the drowning at the ford and the ghost of a grey lady haunting the riverbank and terrace at the rear of the hall may be a vestige of a Lancashire superstition of boggarts. The most famous of these concerned the River Ribble, which took a victim by drowning every year and harks back to a time when the ancient Celts would sacrifice a victim to allay the malevolence of the water demon.

The Bradshaw family of Marple found their chance for prominence during the English Civil War and this is the period when most of the supernatural legends arise. One man in particular, the great judge, John Bradshawe, who tried and condemned King Charles to execution, cast a long shadow over the walls of the gloomy hall and the whole district. In his will he endowed money to a grammar school in Marple, (modelled on one he attended at Middleton in Lancashire), which provided free education for generations of local children, it was finally demolished to make way for the Conservative club on Church Lane.

His brother Henry was an officer in the local Parliamentary militia and supported the seizing of local Royalist's houses, their goods and chattels. After soldiering at sieges and skirmishes in the North West and at one important battle where a bullet smashed his helmet, narrowly missing his skull, he made many local enemies including the Rector of Stockport, Edmund Shallcross who died mysteriously.

There is another ghost, well known to the family, which troubled later Bradshaw Isherwoods. 'Moll of Brabyns', a bitter and disappointed lady who was believed to wander the corridors of the hall invading people's bedrooms. She disliked children and her portrait hanging on the dark and lofty main staircase could not be moved and was thought to be haunted. When the hall was eventually empty and vandalised this painting was cut from its frame and stolen. Did the ghost go with it? Unless the present 'lucky' owner gets in touch and tells us, we shall never know.

John and Henry's father lived quietly in the old black and white Marple Hall until his death in 1654 when Colonel Henry Bradshaw immediately moved in (from Wyberslegh where his large family was living) and started a major rebuilding in stone of the old Tudor framed structure. At the time he was enjoying the spoils of office as a trusted member of the Puritan governing elite. The rebuild was completed in 1658 which is the date proclaimed on the remaining lintel stone – the year of the death of Oliver Cromwell. His brother John had risen to the highest office in the land as Lord President of the Council of State, before being superseded by Cromwell who became a military dictator under the title of Lord Protector. After Cromwell's death John Bradshawe was again briefly Lord President of the Council, but death claimed him also within twelve months and the way was open for the restoration of King Charles II.

Roundheads question Royalists

A visitor to Marple Hall in 1838 described the appearance of the basically 17th century house created by Colonel Bradshaw. Charles Bellairs had made the acquaintance of a young son of the Bradshaw Isherwoods at Oxford (in a period depicted by Jane Austen in her novels), and was invited to stay at the mansion during the summer recess. Though warned by other gentlemen students at the university that the family was considered "peculiar" they had the attraction, to the son of a poor clergyman, of a respectable estate and several unmarried daughters. He was picked up from Manchester by a very large coachman driving a tall antiquated vehicle "the colour of mustard," and after a drive of eleven miles:

"We entered a shabby looking park by a pair of handsome wooden gates with stone pillars and I saw an ample Elizabethan mansion of the sort where an old fashioned country gentleman could live on his four or five thousand a year. The coachman got down and made a great rat tat on the old oaken iron studded front door. It was opened by a stately butler in black who seemed made for the place and the place made for him."

He was welcomed by old Squire Isherwood, a non stop talker, and they entered the antiquated hallway, floored with alternate black and white marble tiles and lit by mullioned leaded windows, some in stained glass with biblical scenes which admitted a dim yellow light. Suits of armour, old paintings, weapons of war and dark oak furniture added to the sombre hue. After a tour of the house he was shown a small closet off a staircase.

King Charles

"This small apartment is vulgarly called by my wife 'King Charles closet'," the old squire informed him. "I do not approve of it myself, but I have to put up with a good many things of which I disapprove. My wife is of a romantic turn and it frequently leads her to excess. That extraordinary and indeed ludicrous figure on its knees is intended for the martyred King Charles perusing his own death warrant." Squire Isherwood then explained the Bradshaw connection. "I am not proud of the connection, though I believe he left considerable wealth to the family. My wife considered that it should be illustrated by that ridiculous figure before you. The wig is made from her own hair. Sir, I am ashamed of it." Charles Bellairs soon married one of Isherwood's daughters and the following year returned for the old man's funeral.

After Henry Bradshaw's rebuild of Marple Hall his son, another Henry, made further additions to the house with tall casement windows and added a brick clock tower to the stables and coachman's cottages, dated 1669.

The last direct Bradshaw male heir died in 1743 and his sister marrying an Isherwood of Bolton, from a family of successful felt makers, the hall and estate passed to the Bradshaw-Isherwoods.

Old oak drawing room

Their son Nathaniel married Elizabeth Brabin (the reputed ghost, Moll of Brabyns) from Brabyns Hall but died without producing an heir. Various successors died young, had ill health or produced no offspring until John Bradshaw Isherwood who in the early 1800s modernised the rear of the hall beside the terrace with bay windows. This was the 'talkative squire' whom Charles Bellairs met. When the old squire died the following year he was succeeded by Bellair's friend Thomas Bradshaw Isherwood, who although he suffered ill health all his life lived to be 75 and sired two children.

His wife Mary Ellen was a forceful woman who in 1842 faced down an angry mob of Luddite strikers who invaded the Park, while carrying an infant daughter in her arms. (This incident was reworked in a novel by the Prime Minister Benjamin Disraeli). Their son John Henry Bradshaw Isherwood took over the estate in the 1880s and installed electricity at the hall. His son Lt. Colonel Frank Bradshaw Isherwood, a professional soldier, was killed near Ypres in WW1, and was the father of famous novelist Christopher Isherwood. John Henry had the distinction of being born in Judge Bradshawe's bed and also dying in it as the Bradshawe room was his bedroom.

From 1929, when most of the contents were sold by auction, caretakers looked after spooky old Marple Hall. They recorded various supernatural occurrences, though visitors were regularly conducted through the rooms, a cafe operated in the summer months and guide books were produced, until the last caretakers left in 1953. Within weeks a chimney stack fell through the roof, and wrecked the main staircase. Soon souvenir hunters were swarming over the property which lay derelict and vandalised for years.

Christopher had finally inherited both Marple and Wyberslegh halls, but as he lived in California resigned them to his younger brother Richard, who still resided at Wyberslegh with his widowed mother Kathleen. Marple Hall was given by Richard to the local Council who demolished it in 1958-59 after the years of neglect and vandalism. Both Christopher and Richard had been victims of haunting episodes at Marple Hall in their infancy and their stories in Chris Isherwood's books are retold here. Christopher described feelings of relief on visiting the cleared site of the hall in the 1960s, "no grimness or sadness, only wonderfully joyful," while a taxi driver waited impatiently for him to finish his final farewell.

Derelict and forlorn after vandalism

Judge and Jury

John Bradshawe who spelled his name with an 'e' was the second son of Henry Bradshaw II the son of the Henry Bradshaw who first came to Marple from Bradshawe Hall near Chapel en le Frith in Derbyshire. His entry of baptism in the Stockport Parish Church register for December 10th 1602 has the added word TRAITOR written in a different hand after the entry.

Humble birthplace of the Judge

There is a tradition that John was born at a small farmstead owned by the Bradshaws called The Place at the bottom of Church Lane, Marple, where the petrol station now stands, bearing a blue plaque erected by Stockport Heritage Trust. His mother died when he was about a year old after giving birth to his brother Francis. John lived with his father at Wyberslegh Hall until he was 17 years old when the family removed to Marple Hall on the death of his grandfather Henry Bradshaw the elder. He was sent to school firstly at Bunbury in Cheshire, where he was taught by Puritan vicar, Edward Burghall, a great believer in driving knowledge in from behind (with the birch) and later at Middleton in Lancashire where similar religious views were instilled in the youth.

As a schoolboy he is said to have scratched a prophetic verse on a gravestone about his destiny which ran:

"My brother Henry must heir the land,

My brother Frank must be at his command,

Middleton Grammar School where he was a pupil

Whilst I poor Jack, will do that, which all the world shall wonder at."

After being articled to an attorney in Congleton he completed his legal education at Gray's Inn and was called to the Bar in 1627 at the age of 25. Returning to Congleton in 1630 he became legal adviser to the Corporation and was made a freeman of the borough. By 1637 he was sufficiently eminent in his profession to be appointed Attorney General for Cheshire, and Congleton honoured him by making him Mayor.

Living in a tall gabled black and white house on the main street with a retinue of servants John Bradshawe began to exhibit, "a lofty domineering tendency" and a determination others should recognise his dignity. Constables, aldermen in their gowns, and "freemen with their halberds" were ordered to accompany him to and from church and on other civic occasions. Whilst in Congleton he married Mary the only daughter of

Young John Bradshawe

John Marbury, squire of Marbury in Cheshire. She was a woman well suited to running an orderly household and kept an eye on her husband's tendency to liberal hospitality and lending money to friends and family without adequate security.

Ominously Mayor Bradshawe ordered that all citizens in Congleton should furnish themselves with sword, helmet and breastplate and exercise in their use with the local Militia.

In 1640 he was appointed Judge of the Sheriffs' Court in London and so entered the metropolitan scene, moving there to live after the outbreak of Civil War between King Charles and the Parliament. His first Parliamentary duty was to help in the prosecution of two Irish rebels, after which he was appointed High Sheriff of Lancashire, a county hotly disputed by the rival forces of King and Parliament.

He also appeared as an advocate before the House of Lords in an appeal on behalf of the democratic orator, John Lilburne, against a conviction for sedition in the King's Star Chamber. Bradshawe established for the first time a defendant's right to silence and overturned the conviction which had seen Lilburne whipped through the streets tied to an ox-cart, for asserting his 'freeborn rights' as an Englishman. Lilburne was awarded compensation by Parliament. But Parliament forgot to pay it.

As war raged up and down the country and trained bands of soldiers shouldering pikes and muskets tramped through the streets of London, Bradshawe continued his legal service, becoming Chief Justice of Chester and North Wales and a Parliamentary Sergeant-at-Law. And when the King was finally defeated and brought to trial by the Army and its junta in Parliament, Bradshawe's name was hurriedly added to a list of 135 commissioners who were to sit in judgement on their monarch.

Judge Bradshawe was one of six commissioners added at the last moment, because nominated peers refused to serve, so it is unlikely that when he was offered the Presidency of the High Court of Justice it had been planned, as several chief justices had refused the 'honour'. "He made earnest apology for himself to be excused, but not prevailing, submitted to their order." He was given the title of Lord President and a retinue of soldiers to protect him, and an official residence in Whitehall during the trial. Secretly an armoured hat was provided for him to wear in case of assassination attempts. This still exists and has been on display at the Hatworks Museum in Stockport. He was fully aware of the danger of his position but determined to do his duty.

The King sat facing John Bradshawe, during the trial, across a long table bearing the Parliamentary mace and sword of state. Row upon row of commissioners who were to judge Charles sat behind Bradshawe also facing the King with their hats on and soberly dressed. Westminster Hall was packed with spectators, and armed soldiers kept them at bay. Underneath his robes Bradshawe also wore further armour as protection against assassination.

When King Charles was brought into the court he sternly viewed the commissioners and the spectators, standing and turning about several times before he sat down. President Bradshawe addressed the prisoner from a raised chair draped in crimson cloth, announcing the court intended to "make inquisition for blood".

As the Attorney General, John Cook, rose to read the charges the King tried to tap him on the arm with his cane, but just then the silver head dropped off. Charles waited, but no-one picked it up so he quickly bent and retrieved it himself. Later he commented to the Bishop of London who saw him in private that it was a bad omen.

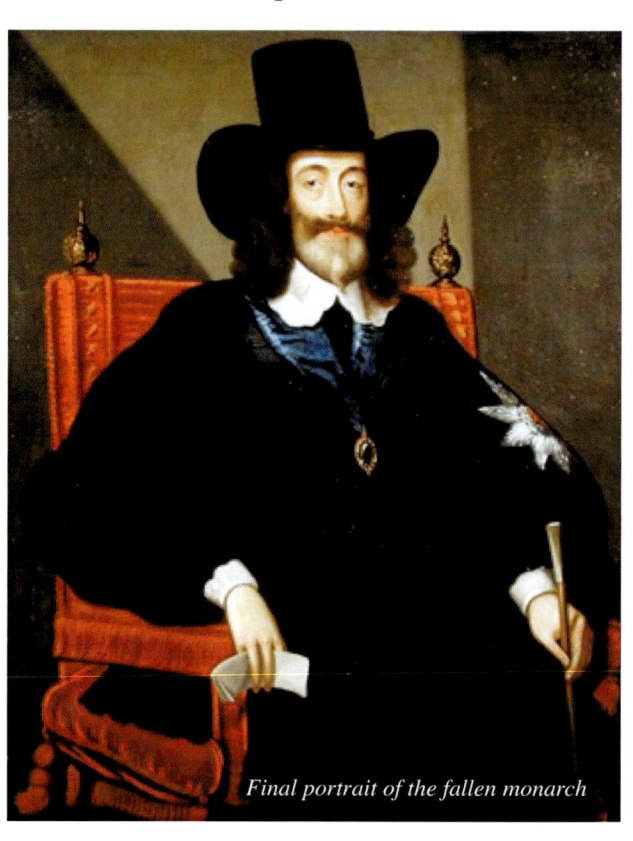

Final portrait of the fallen monarch

Accusing the King of levying Civil War the clerk got to the part wherein he was described as "a tyrant and traitor" Charles, who had remained sternly expressionless, laughed out loud. He denied the validity of the court saying, "remember I am your lawful King, let me know by what lawful authority I am seated here, and you shall hear more from me."

The famous astrologer, William Lilly, who was attending the hearing with Hugh Peters, Cromwell's chaplain, was deeply upset by Bradshawe's attitude to the King as he heard him say: "Sir, instead of answering the Court you interrogate their power, which becomes not one in your condition." Lilly later wrote, "I felt sickened and pierced to my heart to hear a subject thus audaciously reprehend his sovereign, who replied with great magnanimity and prudence."

President Bradshawe insisted that the law was the King's superior in the State and that the People were the authors of the law and had constituted Parliaments for their protection. "And truly Sir you have written your meaning in bloody characters throughout the kingdom!"

But Charles continued to deny the authority of the court comparing it to the illegal power of highway robbers. Embarrassing incidents interrupted the proceedings. One of the commissioners trembling violently called for an adjournment, but

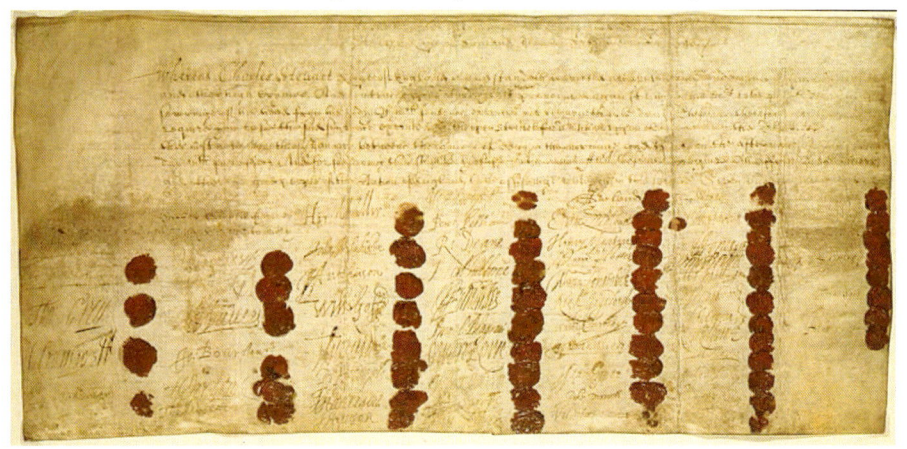

Death Warrant for a King

was browbeaten into silence by Oliver Cromwell, who called him a "froward peevish fellow". Then as Charles was accused of high treason… "for and on behalf of the People of England," a masked lady in the gallery called out: "No, not a hundredth part of them, Oliver Cromwell is a traitor!"

Colonel Axtell in charge of the musketeers was for firing into the gallery, but the lady withdrew, much to the relief of those next to her, which was as well since she turned out to be Lady Fairfax, wife of the Army's Commander in Chief, Lord Fairfax, Oliver Cromwell's nominal boss, who had absented himself from the trial.

Charles was accused of attempting to erect and uphold in himself, "an unlimited and tyrannical power, to rule according to his will and to overthrow the rights and liberties of the people." Evidence was given concerning the battles, destruction and deaths of the first Civil War of 1642, and of Charles deliberately causing the second Civil War of 1648. Their audacity in bringing him to a public trial had stunned the King. He was not a naturally articulate man and suffered from a stammer. Instead of defending his actions he interrogated the court which simply infuriated them.

Having refused to plead or give evidence on his own behalf the hapless monarch was condemned and denied the right to speak after sentence. Bradshawe cried: "Guards withdraw your prisoner!" As Charles was hurried from court he cried out, "I am your king. Think what justice others may have!" The soldiers who hemmed him in jeered and blew tobacco smoke in his face as he passed by. One who blessed him was struck down by Colonel

Axtell. "Poor fellow. A heavy blow for a small offence," commented Charles, who received greater sympathy from people in the crowds lining the public galleries.

In this religious age many believed that God would intervene to save him. The idea of an anointed King being executed was unthinkable. Apart from anything else "to compass or imagine the death of the King" was high treason, as some of the regicides were to find out.

Preparations for the execution were quickly made. The King was allowed to see his younger children in St James Palace where he spent the night. The morning of 30th of January 1649 was frosty and he wore two shirts, "for if I shake with cold, the rogues shall

Bradshawe with his armoured hat

take it for fear". He walked briskly with his guards through St James Park to Whitehall where he rested and took some bread and wine. All the open space around the scaffold outside the Banqueting House, including the roofs of adjacent buildings, and windows with a view of the scene were crowded with spectators.

Several trusted officers had been ordered at short notice by Oliver Cromwell to carry out the preparations and Cromwell wrote and signed their warrant himself. They were Colonels Hacker, Hewson, Axtell, Huncks, and Phayre. All rather grisly sounding names. Subsequently at their trials for regicide they claimed to have been acting under the orders of their superior officer, by the authority of Parliament.

Finding an executioner also proved difficult as the reluctant public executioner, Richard Brandon, had to be brought by a file of soldiers sent by Axtell, along with his axe and a low headsman's block. His assistant had vanished, so a sergeant volunteered as stand in.

Accompanied by Colonel Hacker and his guards the King walked past the crowd of commissioners and favoured spectators inside the Banqueting House, including President Bradshawe and Oliver Cromwell, and stepped through a window which had been removed and onto the scaffold. The headsman and his assistant were wearing bizarre disguises of masks and false beards, the bright axe was leaning near the block, an open coffin lay nearby and several officers and gentlemen witnesses were walking nervously about.

Charles looked at the crowds, the ranks of soldiers drawn up below the scaffold and asked the executioner why the block was so low. "It cannot be higher Sir," he replied. This meant Charles would have to lie full length.

On the platform before his people he then made a speech justifying his actions and declaring his innocence. "I die a martyr for the liberties of England...but the people ought not to have a share in government, that is a thing nothing pertaining to them." A principle most governments have shared since. His own view was that God had brought him to this place for his unfair condemnation of Lord Strafford, a public servant he had sacrificed to the fury of Parliament. He also claimed that he never started the war upon Parliament. "If you look at the date of my commissions and there's you shall see the truth, but I hope God will not hold them to account for it. I believe that ill instruments between them and me are the cause of all this."

Removing his cloak and the St George medallion which he wore around his neck Charles handed them to Bishop Juxon with the simple admonition:"Remember!" Then he lay down, laid his head on the block, prayed for a moment and thrust out his arms. At this signal the executioner brought down the axe severing the King's head with one blow. His assistant caught it, held it up to the crowds and a groan described by one witness as, "such as I never wish to hear again" resounded around Whitehall.

Cromwell's last look at the King

Lord President

Immediately Parliament abolished the office of King and the House of Lords as "unnecessary and dangerous." Cromwell, who went to view the corpse of the King as it lay in Whitehall Palace, was asked as he gazed upon the dead monarch, whose head had been sewn back on, what form of government they would have. "That which is now," he replied.

A Council of State was formed with Cromwell as temporary chairman, but in March, John Bradshawe was formally invested with authority as Lord President of the Council of State. He continued to sit as President of the High Court of Justice and condemned several of the Royalist leaders, captured after their defeat in the Second Civil War, to execution. He was now the effective Head of Government, received foreign ambassadors, issued instructions, signed Acts of Parliament and was given a large salary and the estates of renegade Royalist lords.

During the wars in Ireland and Scotland which soon followed, he and Cromwell kept up a close correspondence. During this honeymoon period Bradshawe wrote to Cromwell: "Truth is, God's blessing upon the wise and faithful conduct of affairs where you are gives life and repute to all other attempts and actions upon the Commonwealth's behalf." He approved the appointment of Cromwell as Commander in Chief of the Army, when Lord Fairfax resigned.

Sometime between 1649 and 1653 Cromwell visited Marple Hall on one of his military expeditions. A guest bedroom at the

Oliver takes a tumble at 'Cromwell's Gig'

hall with heavy beamed gables was shown to later visitors as the room he stayed in, and it is said panelling in the old dining room was specially repainted for the occasion. A ravine in the park near Dooley Lane became known to the family as 'Cromwell's Gig' because the General was thrown from his horse whilst riding across it. The ravine and bridge across it are still there and it is a wonder that "Old Ironsides" survived a tumble here. In old parlance a 'gig' was a whirling object, or a military demotion, which I suppose falling off your horse could be.

Again when Cromwell was sick during his Scottish campaign at Edinburgh, in May 1651, President Bradshawe sent two physicians to attend him, and Oliver wrote profusely thanking the Lord President for his kindness.

English Republicans like Henry Ireton, Cromwell's son in law and lord deputy in Ireland was Bradshawe's friend, but Ireton died of a fever and Cromwell came increasingly under the influence of Army leaders who wanted power for themselves. Differences occurred when Bradshawe took a lenient view of the agitations of Leveller leader, John Lilburne, a prototype socialist whom he had once defended in court, but Cromwell banged the table with his fist declaring: "If you do not break these men in pieces, they will break you!"

After the final battle of the civil wars at Worcester in 1651, when Charles' son Charles II was defeated and fled abroad, Cromwell urged Parliament to start implementing some of the reforms the Council of State had been working on. Instead they merely voted for their own indefinite continuation, provoking him to take radical action. In 1653 Cromwell strode down to the House with a file of musketeers and dissolved Parliament by force.

Then he went to the Council of State and told them they were no longer required. Bradshawe stood up to him:

"Sir we heard what you did at the House in the morning and before many hours all England shall hear it. But Sir you are mistaken to believe that the Parliament is dissolved, for no power under Heaven can dissolve them but themselves. So take you notice of that!"

Later Cromwell described his actions to a close confidant and paid grudging respect when he said: "None gainsaid me save honest John Bradshawe, the President."

Bradshawe's defiance

However Bradshawe was wrong. Briefly Cromwell was popular even with Royalists who thought he would invite Charles II back again. Everyone was sick of the Long Parliament being in unbroken power for over ten years and selling off people's estates to make themselves rich. But they didn't get a king. Cromwell with the help of his chief officers and Parliamentary supporters formed a government with himself as Lord Protector with more power than the king ever had.

So Bradshawe was excluded from the new Protectorate Parliament, but continued his work as Chief Justice of Chester and North Wales. Then when Cromwell died of natural causes in 1658

Bradshawe was elected to Parliament as a Cheshire MP. The Protectorate finally ended with the resignation of Cromwell's son, Richard, from the office he had inherited from his father, and Bradshawe was again made President of the Council of State.

For a few months it seemed as if the Republic was back on track, but Army officers once more started to interfere, and a sick Bradshawe lost patience with one Colonel Sydenham, who was justifying political interference on grounds of divine providence. "Being now going to my God I have not patience to sit here and listen to His great name blasphemed." He got up and left the meeting never to return. Within the month, on Halloween, John Bradshawe died at his London house of a 'tertian ague' - a form of malaria then endemic in Britain, the same disease reputed to have killed Cromwell. Asked on his deathbed if he had regrets about his part in the King's death he replied: "I acted for the good of my country, and had it to be done again I would be the first man in England to do it." Royalists were cock a hoop and said the Devil had taken his soul.

He was given a state funeral, and with pomp and ceremony interred in Westminster Abbey along with the other heroes of the Republic, including Cromwell himself. Uneasy bedfellows they would not rest there for long.

In 1660 after the Restoration of Charles II, various regicides were arrested and tried for their part in the death of his father. The bodies

Cromwell's head

of Bradshawe, Cromwell, and Ireton were disinterred from Westminster Abbey and in January 1661, drawn in their stinking grave wrappings on hurdles through the streets to Tyburn and hanged on the public gallows all day before having their heads struck off, to be stuck on pikes outside Westminster Hall, while their headless trunks were thrown into the common lime pit beneath the gallows.

It is said that a witchlike old hag frightened the soldiers loading the still recognisable corpses in their green and mouldy shrouds onto the sledges prior to taking them to Tyburn, calling out that they should not have been disturbed and that now they were bound to return.

The bequests of President Bradshawe to his native Marple were made null and void by order of a Royalist Parliament. His memory was execrated and the only memorial to him is the blue plaque paid for and erected by Stockport Heritage Trust on the petrol station near the site of his reputed birthplace in Church Lane. Yet he is the most famous son ever to come out of Marple, or Stockport.

His kinsman, the regime's Latin secretary and poet, John Milton wrote his epitaph: "A faithful and unfailing friend, he assisted the deserving to the utmost of his power. If the cause of the oppressed was to be defended, if the favour or violence of the great was to be withstood, it was impossible to find an advocate more intrepid or more eloquent – one no threats and terrors, and no rewards could seduce from the plain path of rectitude."

Colonel of Marple

While his younger brother John was reaching the pinnacle of national prestige, Henry Bradshaw III the young squire was carrying on the life of an aspiring country gentleman in dangerous times. Early in the Civil War his Puritan religious convictions led him to enlist as a captain in Robert Duckenfield's regiment based around Stockport.

He was probably at the sieges of the Royalist held halls at Adlington and Wythenshawe, or the battles at Middlewich and Nantwich in 1643. Being only a year older than John he would have taken an active part, as a man in his prime. When Colonel Duckenfield's regiment failed to stop the advance of a 10,000 strong army led by Prince Rupert after a skirmish at Cheadle and Stockport in May 1644, Captain Bradshaw was likely among the

Parliamentarians who beat a hasty and ignominious retreat towards Manchester.

Rupert skirted Manchester and left the heavily defended town alone, heading for the softer target of Bolton where a massacre of townsfolk and children was perpetrated by the troops of the Earl of Derby who ran amok. Passing into Yorkshire the Royalist army was annihilated at the Battle of Marston Moor by the united forces of Parliament and the Scots.

On Duckenfield's return to Stockport, after their recent fright, a committee of sequestration was set up to fine 'delinquents' - that is people suspected of having helped the Royalists. Two prominent victims were William Davenport of Bramall Hall, and Edmund Shallcross, the rector of Stockport. Henry Bradshaw was appointed a commissioner of sequestration and sent out agents assisted by soldiers. Davenport described how the soldiers surrounded his house with loaded muskets, their matches lit ready to fire. The agents ransacked every room and made an inventory, demanding to know what was

Staircase House, home of Elizabeth Shallcross

in every box and chest. Those horses the Royalists had spared him were then taken away and he was fined.

Reverend Shallcross had a library of over 600 books which were seized, but his sister in law bought them back for him. A complete inventory was made of the contents of his rectory including curtains hidden in a box in the chimney of his wife's bedroom. His brother John Shallcross was a Royalist colonel fighting for the King, yet Elizabeth Shallcross, John's wife, who rescued his books was a keen Puritan with brothers fighting for Parliament. She could not save Edmund being ejected from his comfortable living, and may even have approved of the Puritan minister, Samuel Eaton, Duckenfield's chaplain, who replaced him.

It is said that Shallcross was also in a private dispute with Henry Bradshaw over the collection of church tithes in Marple,

Haunted corridor in Staircase House

and that this influenced his treatment. He made several trips to London to appeal against his sequestration. On the last visit he and his Parliamentary escort of cavalry were attacked by cavaliers from Dudley Castle and the unlucky clergyman was killed.

Sometime around then the legend of the cavalier who visited Marple Hall, never to be seen again, was born. It is claimed that a young Royalist was in love with a daughter or niece of Henry Bradshaw III called Esther. He visited the Hall and stayed the night, but secretly Henry's wife had his saddlebags searched where documents incriminating to the family were found. A scuffle may have taken place on the main staircase which had an indelible bloodstain, caused it is said by a sword wound. A servant then guided the cavalier and his horse to a pool of the River Goyt,

The Mere Pool in 17th C.

claiming to show him a safe place to cross. In he plunged and as horse and rider were swept downstream his horrified lover spied the scene from the windows of the hall. She rushed down and crying distractedly ran along the riverbank, but of her lover there was neither sight nor sound.

Henry had been promoted to Major and was with Duckenfield at the surrender of the Royalist city of Chester. He was then made Lt. Colonel in Colonel Ashton's regiment and later ordered to raise a militia regiment in the Macclesfield Hundred. He instructed the Constable at Marple to guard the roads and turn away those without a password or written permission to travel, and his requisitioning horses from local people to carry ammunition created violent opposition. After ordering a muster of men barely 40 turned up and many sent excuses. He confided in letters to his brother that he wished he could resign, but raids by cavaliers from Derbyshire prevented this. While the Bradshaws were becoming more powerful, they were also becoming resented and unpopular.

'Ironsides' advance at Worcester

In 1651 the North West was alarmed at the news of a Scottish army under Charles II advancing through Preston. The militia was called out and a list of some names of Col. Henry Bradshaw's regiment is preserved in Earwaker's history 'East Cheshire', including some of my own relatives the Fowdens who were junior officers. After being harassed by Cromwell's men on the march through Lancashire, King Charles made a dash south, concentrating his forces at Worcester. Cromwell, now reinforced by militia regiments including Henry Bradshaw's, attacked via a series of improvised bridges over the River Severn.

It was a disaster for the Scots and the Royalist cause. Colonel Bradshaw was injured by a bullet which struck his helmet as he led his regiment forward, and about a dozen men of his regiment were killed or wounded, but Cromwell secured a victory. The

Colonel Henry Bradshaw was wounded

damaged helmet was displayed for years afterwards at Marple Hall, along with the sword he carried. The scattered Royalists fled and young Charles evaded capture disguised as a woodsman in ill fitting shoes, and by hiding in an oak tree while Roundhead soldiers searched beneath.

The Earl of Derby was among the Royalist prisoners and he was sent for trial by court martial at Bolton, where his troops had massacred townsfolk. Cromwell ordered Col. Bradshaw to sit as a commissioner on the trial after which Derby was beheaded on the Market Place at Bolton.

This was the last battle of the civil wars and Cromwell called it "a crowning mercy."

Colonel Henry Bradshaw then started the major rebuilding in stone of Marple Hall on the death of his father in 1654, creating the hall completed in 1658 which stood for just 300 years. It's likely the stone for this was quarried from the steep rock at the rear of the hall, which still shows signs of extraction. As a keen Puritan, believing in the work ethic, he worked hard on his estate and as a local magistrate. He is credited with replacing an

Old quarry behind Marple Hall

old wooden bridge over Otterspool on the Goyt with a two arched stone bridge joining the villages of Romiley and Marple.

He made frequent business trips to Stockport and Manchester to buy domestic supplies as his account books testify, and patronised hostelries around the Market Place. He made less frequent trips to Macclesfield and doubtless was visited by his famous brother, the judge, on John's circuit of his legal duties in Chester and North Wales after he lost the Lord Presidency. The judge's impressive carved canopied bed was preserved at Marple Hall in the Bradshawe room, and is said to have been brought there from Wyberslegh.

Unlike the Lord President, Henry was still alive when the tables were turned and Charles II was restored to his throne. He was called to account for his

Judge Bradshawe's carved oak bed

part in the death of the Earl of Derby. In a humble petition for pardon before the House of Lords he pleaded in mitigation that he was at the trial by order of his General, that he did not sign the death warrant, that he had interceded with the court's president to try to save the earl's life, and at the request of the earl he had written to his brother, the Lord President to save him.

Bradshaw told them he was, "a poor man, in debt, with a small estate, a poorly wife and a large family of eleven children" and he, "humbly craved his gracious majesty's pardon, and that his errors might be imputed to his lamented ignorance and mistake." By such grovelling many of the old regime managed to hang onto their lives and estates, instead of hanging and losing them. They survived the transition, whereas many loyal Royalists who had faithfully served King Charles regained nothing.

After about a month in prison he was liberated on the payment of various fines, but became ill and died the following year, the shock having unsettled him, being buried in the Bradshaw vault at Stockport Parish Church. The Bradshaw family, as we know, continued to live at Marple Hall.

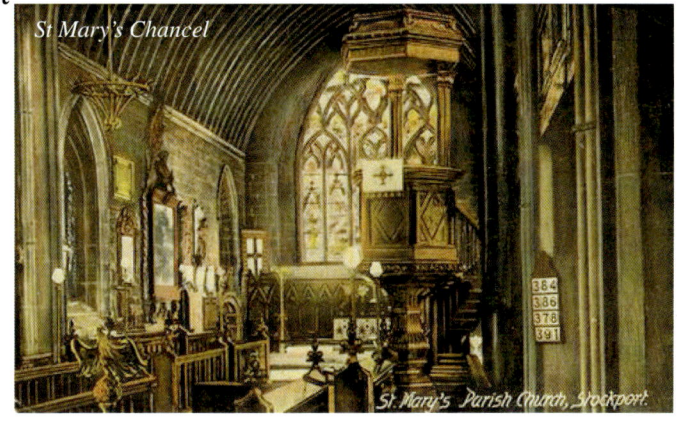

Grey Lady at the stile

Grey Lady

So Henry Bradshaw unlike his brother the Judge, who died childless, had many sons and several daughters. Thanks to the law of primogeniture the estates passed down through elder sons until the elder male line failed and Isherwoods acquired Marple Hall by marriage to an heiress. But there are many direct male line descendants of Henry Bradshaw through his younger sons. My own relatives the Fowdens, a local farming family, were related to a collateral branch.

Local people used to know all about the story of the grey lady who haunted the woods leading down to the riverbank. Even Christopher Isherwood in his account of the hauntings

Mere Pool today

referred to her haunting the 'Lady Wood' and the terrace behind the hall. His version claimed that she had been driven insane by the sight of her cavalier lover drowning, which she is said to have seen from the hall. He also referred to the Mere Pool below the hall being drained in 1810 and an old Civil War type helmet, spurs and a horse's bridle bit being recovered, supposedly proving the story.

The problem is that the Mere Pool is now a silted up pond below the terrace within sight of the hall, while the river is a considerable distance away and more or less impossible to see, even if we assume the tall trees blocking the view were not then grown up. Perhaps the river was diverted and partially drained for

Bridle bit, stirrups, and Civil War armour on mantelpiece

the building of the now collapsed weir at Chadkirk (near the present cyclists' bridge) around about 1800. This is close to the old ford and maybe in those days it was called the Mere Pool (which means lake pool and is said to be how Marple, *Mer pul* got its name). The valley was probably much more marshy then, with pools full of fish, hence its attraction for otters as in 'Otterspool' by the road bridge and garden centre. And it is exciting to hear that otters have recently returned to the Goyt, attracted by salmon and trout, but you'll have to guess where.

Harry Cotton writing in a guide book of the 1930s claimed the Mere Pool was once a large lake forming part of the river and stretching as far as the terrace behind the hall. Even so young Esther must have had very good eyesight, or the tale is a partial version of events. As it involves the bloodstain on the staircase

A cavalier's final journey to Mere Pool?

and a caretaker prone to seeing ghosts running screaming from the hall one day shouting, "they're fighting on the stairs!", perhaps the actual basis of the story was more complicated.

Folktales often preserve an element of truth long after the participants have taken their secrets to the grave. My own guess is that if the poor young cavalier died 'resisting arrest', his useful horse was requisitioned by the Roundhead army, and his personal items along with the body were disposed of. No need to carry it too far with a lake behind the house, and wearable ironmongery to weigh it down. The identity assigned to this unfortunate in the folktale was a son of the Leghs of High Legh in Cheshire, although a later Henry Bradshaw did marry a daughter of Richard Legh of High Legh after the Civil War, without objections being raised.

This inconsistency never stopped local people seeing the grey lady. I have spoken to at least three people with sightings in the area. First of all my grandmother, Alice Cliffe neé Fowden, as a girl living at Clapgate Farm a little way down the valley at Bredbury Green, had several sturdy brothers who when the day's labours were done wended their way through the woods past Marple Hall to slake their thirst in Marple hostelries. They all saw, or thought they saw, a grey shape by a stile in the woods, which then glided silently away. On another occasion a figure ran screaming from the hall, which was shut up and supposedly empty, prompting Tommy to swear he'd never walk that way again.

Another sighting was close by the old Stag and Pheasant alehouse near Otterspool Bridge, reported by a reader of the Stockport Heritage Magazine, which I edited for many years. Now a rather attractive private house in russet stone, it was once a hedge alehouse frequented by pedlars, burglars and highway robbers, several of whom were members of the notorious Oldham family who lived at Boggart House, a lonely spot beside the Goyt. My reader was driving past one night when her car headlights picked out the flowing skirts of the grey lady as she flittered across the road, disappearing from sight through a stone wall. (It so happens that there is a narrow stile in the wall here allowing walkers to access the old cobbled and overgrown route from Bredbury Green).

Old stable cottages where Arthur spotted the ghost

The best account of this ghost is by Arthur Brindley a native of Marple who as a young man during the 1930s and 40s rented a cottage in the old stables at Marple Hall, when the hall was tenanted by caretakers. "Dunna be surprised if you see some queer things here, there's always something going on," the old caretaker told him after a couple of drinks.

Busily decorating his new cottage Arthur was up a ladder one day when he saw a lady on the terrace at the rear of the hall, looking over a stone balustrade above the valley. "She had dark hair and a white dress – but I could see through her! I came down that ladder quickly and shouted my friend Harold to come and see. Then she turned and seemed to glide along and went through a door at the rear of the hall. Harold went to look, but he never saw a thing," said Arthur.

Grey Lady on the terrace

Soon afterwards a new caretaker and his wife, Mr and Mrs C. moved into the hall. "Mrs C. told me that the first night they were there she woke up and through the door came a lady to the bottom of the bed. Mrs C. nudged 'Jack' but he didn't wake up and the lady just smiled and went back through the door. This was the ghost of an older lady," said Arthur, "the one I saw was a young woman."

A travelling salesman from Cadbury's also told Arthur that on a visit to the hall he found the caretaker in a state of terror rushing out of the building and shouting about ghostly figures, "they're fighting, they're fighting on the staircase!" Inside they found nothing going on but the caretaker insisted he had seen "a cavalier and three men". Some friends of Arthur also did a ghost watch inside the hall on a particular date until midnight when, "a wind rattled the windows and the head and shoulders of a woman floated into the room, across it and into another room," by which time they were all tumbling out of the building.

Arthur said Richard Isherwood, the hall's owner, told him that the ghost of the older woman was supposed to be Elizabeth Brabin who was looking for a lost wedding ring. She was thought to dislike children being in the house. The younger woman was a daughter or niece of one of the Cromwellian Bradshaws, whose Royalist lover had been drowned in the Goyt, which then ran below the hall – it was later diverted for the Chadkirk printworks.

He had been attacked on the staircase of the hall by three Bradshaws claimed Richard after it was discovered he carried warrants for their arrest. A bloodstain in the polished wooden boards on the first landing, shown to later generations of visitors, was caused when he slashed one of his assailants on the leg with his sword. The gentleman's name was Legh of High Legh near Lymm in Cheshire and he met his death supposedly by the treachery of a servant who misdirected him across a deep part of the Goyt shortly after this struggle.

Arthur Brindley became an antique dealer and bought and sold various items which Richard Isherwood had inherited. Among those he kept was a carved antique chest of 17th C. date and a basket hilted Civil War broadsword, perhaps the very one Colonel Bradshaw carried at the battle of Worcester. Both lay in Arthur's bedroom next to the carved oak bed, also from Marple Hall in which as an old man he used to sleep. I interviewed Arthur at his cottage in Disley for Stockport Heritage Magazine in 1989, when he was in his eighties. He said he never missed a wink of sleep and had never seen a ghost since.

Caretaker Harry Cotton, and Frank Tunstall's guidebooks describe various interesting features of the old Hall. One was a description of Judge Bradshawe's bedroom, which contained a large heavily carved tester bed with a canopy. This was on the first floor near the

Oliver Cromwell

main staircase and had stained glass windows inscribed with his prophetic schoolboy rhyme predicting his future greatness. The bed was carved with the motto: "He that is unmercilful shall mercy miss: But he shall have mercy that merciful is." Another on the inside of the canopy read: "Love God not gold," and "Sleep not until U consider how U have spent the time: If well, thank God, if not, repent."

The higher staircase held a portrait of Elizabeth Brabin weeping beside an open grave, supposedly of her young husband, Nathaniel Bradshaw-Isherwood, which as she was childless, robbed her of the chance to continue as Lady chatelaine of Marple Hall. At the very top of the staircase was a room leading to the roof, below which a priest's hole or passage was found during alterations in the early 19th century, containing two skeletons. A shaft led from here down to the cellars and may have provided a secret escape route. In two of the old bedrooms at this level were curious canopies and the remains of a niche possibly for a statue (of a saint?).

A narrow twisting stair led down to the ground floor and the old dining room, where it is said Oliver Cromwell ate on his visit to the house. Fastened on wooden panels to the side of the fireplace were two old muzzle loading gun racks, where loaded firearms could have been placed to keep their powder dry and out of the way of chance sparks! Oliver always slept with armed bodyguards at his bedroom door, and never in the same bed twice. Likewise he often changed his intended routes and frustrated many assassination attempts by such means. One of his favourite sayings was: "Put your trust in God and keep your powder dry!"

Caretaker Harry Cotton believed that the cottages by the stable block were built to house Henry Bradshaw's Roundhead troopers and that the date of 1669 on the brick built clocktower was a later addition to the sandstone cottages. These included the cottage from whence Arthur Brindley saw the Grey Lady, and where he held many lively parties as a young man in the 1930s-40s, while he worked at Avros in Woodford. Harry Cotton ended his 1934 guidebook with a rather good piece of poetic prose:

Clocktower on the stable block

"Time changes all things, and we must always change with them. Yet, one can hardly look back on the old grey walls of Marple Hall without a mingled feeling of sadness, when it is remembered that hundreds of years have passed since the close of those sterling days.

"Like a play that has ended, the hall is the stage; now deserted and silent. Now, as then, the bell in the old clocktower still strikes out the hour at midnight, and its soft mellow tone,

ringing out through the woods and valleys, tells of the passing of another day.

"As the bell ceases to resound and stillness reigns again, a faint echo of the last stroke can be heard from across the dale, as if in answer from the long dim past: and who shall blame the spirits of the departed if they, at the solemn hour when night and morning meet, revisit their old haunts in the lower world, which was once their home. The stern old Puritan Colonel, and the grim visage of the Lord President."

Marple Hall memorial stone

Were their shades to return to the grassy mounds, banks of weeds and a feeble outline of stones which was once the romantic old hall, there would be little of those old haunts they would recognise today.

A strange Haunting

Tis said as when the moon's bright beams,
Illumine Marple's Hall.
A headless form is seen to glide,
Along the oaken wall.

There was a dark panelled corridor in Marple Hall leading past the Judge's bedroom which family members believed to be haunted by the headless ghost of Charles I, the unlucky monarch Lord President Bradshawe had sentenced to death, showing little of that mercy spoken of in the inscription on his bedstead.

Oak corridor

But it was another ghost – that of a family member by marriage which seemed to most exercise the imaginations of subsequent generations of Bradshaw Isherwoods. On the top flight of the main staircase hung an unframed oil painting on stretched canvas of an 18th century lady dressed in black, wearing a white kerchief on her head and with a black and white floppy eared dog like a spaniel pawing on her lap. This harsh-featured gentlewoman was said to be Elizabeth Brabin, wife of Nathaniel the first of the Bradshaw Isherwoods.

Nathaniel died in1765 leaving no heir as the marriage was childless. Marple Hall estate passed to his brother Thomas, and Elizabeth returned to her father's house, Brabyns Hall, on the other side of Marple. She was supposed to have resented the loss of Marple so passionately that her ghost came back to haunt it, restlessly searching for her wedding ring. Curiously her portrait showed the lady without a wedding ring. "Moll" as she was nicknamed was believed to resent children as usurpers of 'her' property. She wanted to scare them off the premises and was seen by several generations of young family members.

Maids disliked moving the picture for cleaning, as strange knocking and creaking noises in the old hall invariably followed. In the summer of 1907 while his parents Kathleen and Frank were away on holiday from Wyberslegh, Christopher Isherwood who was then almost 3 years old and his Nanny went to stay at Marple Hall in the big NE room at the top of the hall. On the first night Christopher awoke after midnight and complained loudly to his nurse of "the muzzy old woman sitting on the end of my bed. I don't like her Nanny, no I don't."

Sure enough the experience was repeated every night at about the same time. The Nanny woke each time in a sweat, thoroughly alarmed as creaking and knocking noises accompanied the phenomena and though she saw nothing, said she felt a third presence in the room. Christopher meanwhile gave a running commentary on

Kathleen with baby Christopher

the ghost's movements, "now she's going down the steps," or "out of the window."

Christopher and the 'haunted' painting

Frank, Christopher's father, who as a professional soldier had seen action in the Boer War and was to be killed leading his men in WW1, was entirely convinced that Christopher had seen Moll of Brabyns. So it is strange that when the couple left for a further five week holiday in Spain later that year Christopher and Nanny were again lodged in the haunted bedroom at Marple Hall.

This next occurrence was more complicated. Christopher had been left fast asleep in his cot, the sides of which were up, with just a night light burning and the bedroom door shut. Nanny went to get her supper, asking the maid in the room next door to go to him if he awoke and called out. As they were finishing supper the maid came down and said there had been no sound in the nursery. Just then they heard a strange noise outside on the haunted terrace at the rear of the house, like a shuffling and deep sighing. A moment later Christopher's voice was heard in the anteroom to the servants hall calling, "Nanny".

She ran to the door and found him standing on the cold stone floor in bare feet wearing only his nightshirt, yet when she picked him up he was still warm. Asked how he got there he said, "Daddy came, popped the lights on and carried me down." Both his parents were then in Spain. Somehow he had let down the side of his cot, opened a big heavy door, come down two flights of stairs, gone along a stone passage and across a stone hall and was still quite warm on a cold late October evening. Then things got even stranger.

Christopher with his Nanny

    As he was taken upstairs back to bed Nanny was surprised to see through a gap above the door a bright light in the bedroom and something moving against it. On attempting to go in they found the door firmly jammed from the inside. They fled downstairs and Christopher's grandfather and uncle Jack were summoned. Jack managed to force the door open a little way and discovered that a chair was wedged between it and the chest of drawers beside the doorway. The lights had been turned on and the sides of the cot let down, an impossible thing for Christopher to do.

Jack later speculated that some "guardian angel" had taken on the form of Frank in order that the child should not be frightened and removed Christopher from a malign presence in the room, which had meant him harm. What was done to the door, lights and cot, was to ensure that notice would be taken. The idea of some hoaxer arranging all this then climbing out of the window and down the ivy, possibly falling, accounting for the sighing and shuffling heard on the terrace was rejected as too elaborate a plot.

Grandma, Grandpa, Richard and Christopher

When Christopher was older he used to examine the chest of drawers and demonstrate to himself how the door had been jammed by the chair, but he could not elicit in the slightest degree any memory of what had really happened to him on October 29th 1907.

It was different with his brother Richard. In late October of the year 1914 Kathleen who had come up to Marple from London noted in her diary that Richard, "has begun to see the old woman who haunted Christopher at his age." Richard was seven years

Main staircase Marple Hall

younger than Christopher and the correspondence of late October dates was very close. As Kathleen sat with Richard looking at a picture book of steam trains she asked him if the old woman had said anything to him.

He replied, "she says 'you *muſt* go away' and she come and look at me in bed, and I say 'I don't want to go away' and she say 'Oh but you *muſt*'!" Kathleen arranged that he and Nanny move into another bedroom and it seems strange that they had been put into the haunted room in the first place. But when Nanny and the servants realised that Richard had been disturbed by something in the room they told him the story of Moll and the painting.

Nearly 40 years later Christopher discovered the alarming sequel to this story when he and Richard were discussing their perplexing experiences as children:

Richard: "I didn't tell Mummy what really happened. I said it was an old woman for the sake of peace, because I wanted to leave the room next day. I was afraid she wouldn't believe me."

Christopher: "Then you didn't see anything? You mean nothing happened?"

Richard: "Oh dear no, I didn't mean that at all! I didn't see an old woman. I saw a dressmaker's dummy."

Christopher: A dressmaker's dummy! But… did it have a head?"

Richard: "No, not a head exactly. There was some kind of screw sticking out of the top of it… It looked so funny, with the screw sticking out of it, jumping up and down."

Christopher: "It had feet then?"

Richard: "I don't know, I couldn't see. I could only see the upper part of its body. I suppose it had feet. You see, when it jumped up and down, I could hear the noise of feet on the wooden floor."

Christopher: "Where was this thing when you saw it?"

Richard: "It was near the door."

Christopher: "Was the door open?"

Richard: "Oh dear no, the door was locked. It had got in through the locked door. That was what terrified me."

Christopher: "Did you scream?"

A very strange haunting!

Richard: "No I didn't scream. I tried to wake Nanny though. But I couldn't, she was sound asleep."

Christopher: "Did it speak to you?"

Richard: "Oh no. I don't think it saw me thank goodness. Well, not exactly. But it made me feel it knew I was there. And it wanted to drive me away. It was threatening me."

Christopher: "And you made that up to tell Mummy in the morning?"

Richard: "Well I had to tell her something. I couldn't tell her I saw a dressmaker's dummy, could I? Of course I don't expect you to believe me Christopher. But I can't help it, that's what happened."

Christopher tried cross questioning Richard one evening when he was drunk, but couldn't discover inconsistencies in his story. Surely Richard must have dreamt it, he reasoned? But Richard wouldn't be shaken and slowly Christopher realised that his brother genuinely believed what he saw and heard on that October night to have been a real and terrifying experience.

Christopher slept in most of the bedrooms at Marple Hall over the course of summer holidays and when he was alone at night there was always a background of fear in his

Staircase wrecked by chimney stack

mind. Fear that the something which had manifested itself once might manifest again at any moment. In certain rooms the sense of psychic menace was related to some feature, like the darkened beams of the gable embedded in the wall of Cromwell's apartment. He got used to the sense of menace as one would accustom to the presence of wild animals in the jungle at night.

Without doubt he believed in the supernatural happenings at Marple Hall and didn't find them Halloweenish or fun, they were squalid, he felt, and a public offence like bad drains. It was a sick house, a psychic slum, and ought to be burned down. He didn't feel like that about Wyberslegh, which no-one claimed to be haunted. But even without his ill wishes, Marple Hall was doomed.

When uncle Henry Isherwood inherited Marple in 1929 he sold most of the contents in a public auction on the premises. Caretakers looked after the half empty house for the next twenty odd years. Even after it was almost completely empty in 1953 and the chimney stack collapsed through the main staircase, the portrait of Moll of Brabyns still hung on the wall above. Later that year Richard found it taken down and leaning against the stairs half torn from the wooden stretcher. Richard hung it up again. A few days later he found it lying rolled up in the Glory Hole minus the stretcher. A few days later and it disappeared. Richard and Christopher wondered if the ghost went with it?

Within a few months the hall was systematically wrecked. Lead drain pipes were ripped off the walls and windows smashed, woodwork on the staircase hacked to pieces and even a bathtub half dragged down the back staircase. The brothers who by now owned the derelict went to look at it and saw a gutted ruin, stripped of its ivy, with black staring window holes. They went inside and found a pink marble fireplace uncle Henry had brought back from Italy intact, but that was all. When they came out quite a few sightseers were wandering peaceably about, taking photographs. It suddenly occurred to Christopher that he and Richard had also become Marple Hall ghosts! But no-one screamed.

Christopher and Richard 1960

Epilogue

Years ago the Manchester Evening News carried an article about a caravan struck by lightning on Werneth Low, in which I was writing a piece for Stockport Heritage Magazine about the hauntings at Marple Hall.

I had just got to the bit about the painting of a woman weeping at her husband's grave when the keyboard of my old manual typewriter was blotted out in a flash of light and terrific clap that rocked the caravan, blowing all the windows and rooflights open. The home of my antiquarian friend John Oldham and his five cats acted as a Faraday cage, which saved us, the charge passing harmlessly around us, but heating up and shattering the globes of his gaslight brackets frightening the cats as it did so.

Recently when writing the book you are reading, I got to the passage that mentions Christopher Isherwood's "guardian angel." A fault in my laptop's keyboard promptly and unaccountably repaired itself and all the non-functioning keys started working properly. This had never happened before in the five years I've owned it, and ceased next time I switched it on, as it reverted to the usual malfunction. It struck me as odd. I had spent the entire day writing the last chapter and stuck my head out to find that the hamlet I live in had been cut off by floods and the only bridge in and out trashed, for the first and only time in living memory.

Worse, the nearby town of Whaley Bridge had been evacuated amid fears of a collapse of the dam on Toddbrook Reservoir. So there we have another synchronicity of Marple Hall – ghost story, keyboard, and extreme weather event. Though I accept no responsibility for the consequences.

Some years ago I was approached by a reader of the magazine who said that she had been a psychic medium from childhood and was so sensitive to atmospheres that she was unable to enter Staircase House, the restored medieval townhouse on Stockport Market Place. But she would like to if accompanied, in case she became strongly affected by the place.

Three sympathetic members of Stockport Heritage accompanied her and all went well until we entered the 17th century room at the rear of the staircase. A painting of a gentleman in a grizzled periwig caught her attention, when she became distressed and started to talk to him, telling him not to worry and that his house was being looked after.

A member of staff who had been watching the commotion on CCTV dashed into the room by which time she was in tears and holding out both her hands in supplication to the jolly looking dandy in the portrait, who seemed to us quite unmoved. Later she explained that he had told her

The 'talking' painting

he was very worried about his house and kept repeating, "What have they done to my house? Oh, what have they done to my beautiful house?" She reassured him that it was now being taken care of, thinking he meant Staircase House. She was not to know that the gentleman in the painting was a Bradshaw Isherwood, and that the portrait had been purchased with others from the auction sale at Marple Hall and had nothing to do with Staircase House.

These are the stories and folk tales about Marple Hall which have been handed down over centuries. I merely retell the sayings of others. You must make up your own mind as to what it all means, and if you ask me whether I have an explanation for ghosts I shan't answer with confidence, as we all have our own views, but say with Shakespeare: *"There are more things in Heaven and Earth, Horatio, than are dreamt of in your philosophy."*

Steve Cliffe, Oct. 2019

(60 years since Marple Hall was demolished)

Places to visit

Marple Hall -There are lots of places to visit in the borough connected with the story of Marple Hall. The footpaths around the site of the hall still trace out the route where the Bradshaws and Cromwell would have ridden through the park, and Cromwell's Gig, where he fell off his horse, can be seen, not that much different in appearance from what it once was. (The Mere Pool and dangerous broken steps down to it still exist, but these are on private property so should be avoided). You can walk to the old ford over the River Goyt just downstream from the new cycleway bridge to Chadkirk, where the young cavalier should have crossed in safety from the Marple side. The cobbled way leading from Marple Hall Drive can be seen, regularly traversed by dog walkers without a second glance. Most people now associate 'Marple Hall' with the adjacent school, built on land which was once part of the Bradshaw Isherwood's private park. But the grass grown outline of old masonry, with a lintel stone and plaque put up by Marple Civic Society, are all that remain of the once great hall.

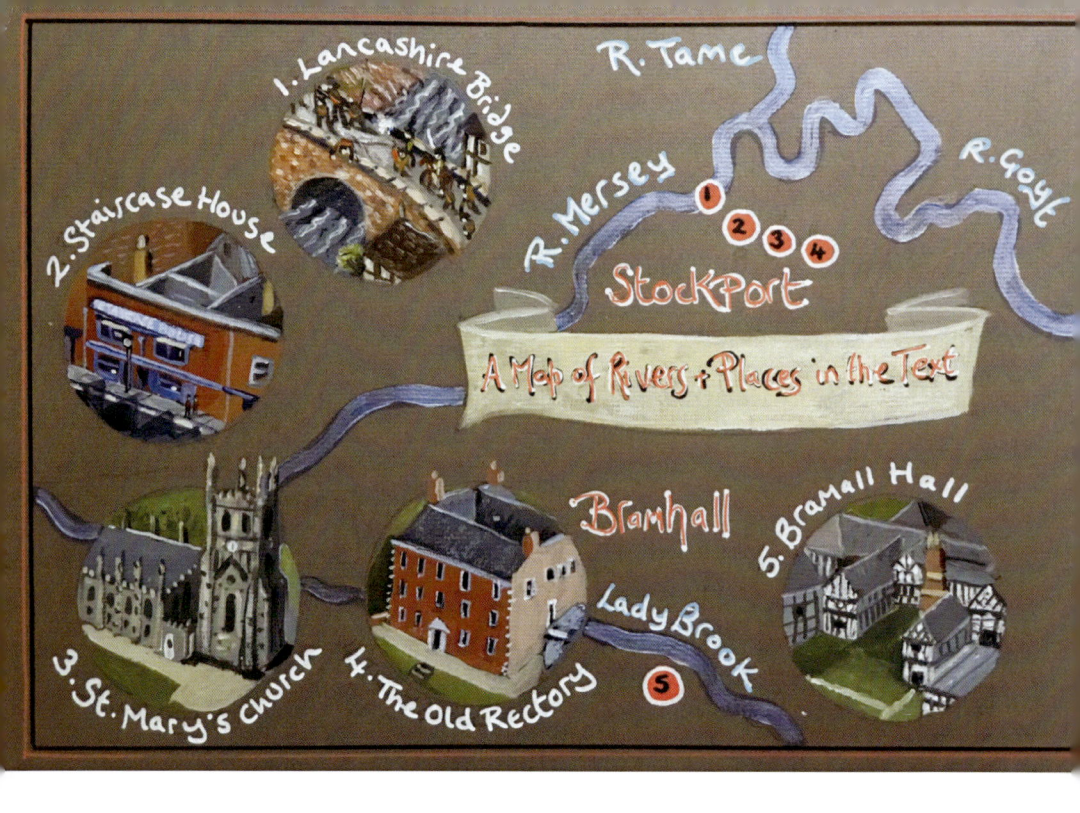

Wyberslegh Hall- The other ancestral hall still stands in High Lane and the rear which faces the road has been converted into private houses, while the front, hidden from the road by trees, is still empty. It is of timber framed construction clad in stone. Christopher and Richard lived here as children and Richard lived there with his mother until she died in 1960. By that time it had become very damp and run down. The ashes of Kathleen and Richard are in the garden.

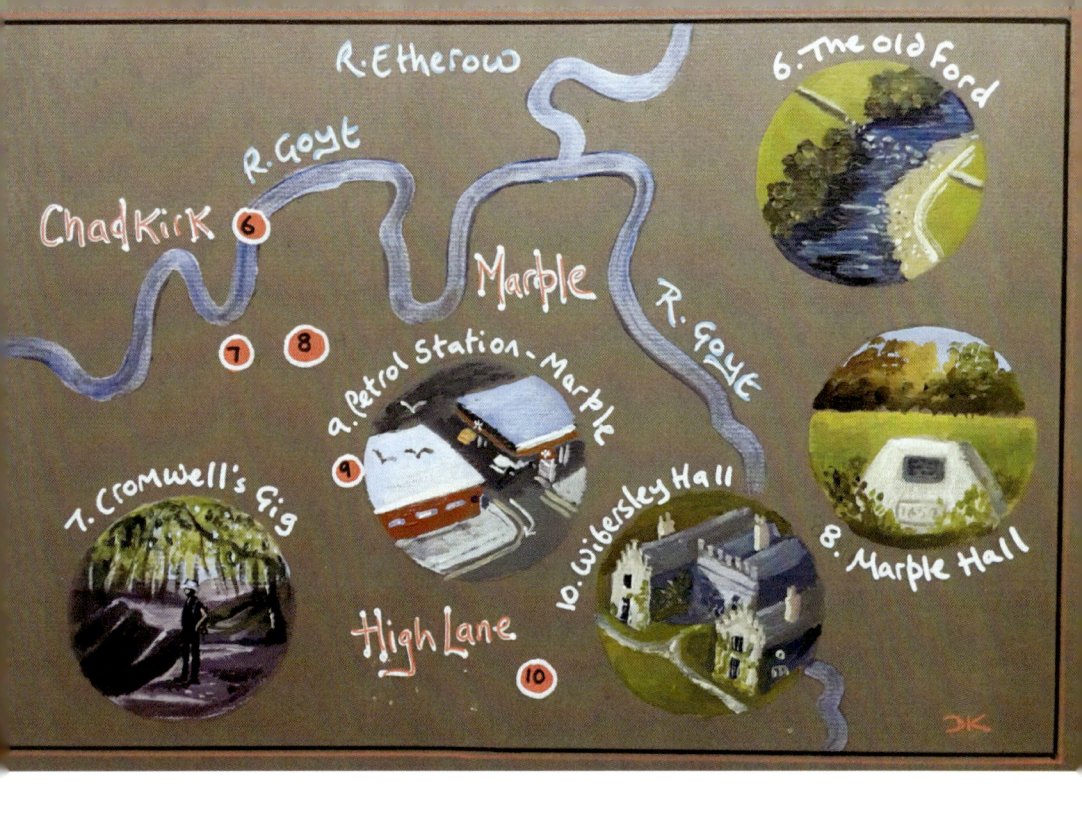

Petrol Station- Church Lane, Marple, is the site of The Place, otherwise Peace Farm, another timber framed house clad in brick or stone and reputedly the birthplace of Judge Bradshawe when his father was farming the neighbouring fields, now entirely built up. This area was known at one time as Norbury Smithy. There is a blue plaque by Stockport Heritage Trust commemorating the 'Lord President' erected on the wall of the present building.

Otterspool Bridge- Rebuilt in stone by Col. Henry Bradshaw at the height of his prosperity probably using stone from his quarry for the rebuilding of Marple Hall. Nearby is the old former Stag and Pheasant alehouse and the old cobbled way to Bredbury Green in the woods opposite, which Cromwell would have ridden up to visit the Ardernes of Arden Hall, Bredbury, hence its nickname of 'Cromwell's Castle'.

Chadkirk Chapel- The old chapel once belonging to the Davenports was derelict at one time and used for stabling horses. Independent puritan soldiers of Henry Bradshaw and their families started religious meetings here and after the Restoration, having been ejected, opened the first Hatherlow Chapel nearby. Chadkirk Chapel is open at weekends and 'Friends of Chadkirk' tend the gardens and organise a well dressing annually.

St. Mary's Church- Stockport Parish Church where the Bradshaws were baptised and buried is on the Market Place in central Stockport. Soldiers killed at the Battle of Stockport in May 1644 were buried here. The old chancel and vestry are part of the original church and house a heritage centre run by Stockport Heritage Trust volunteers on market days. The Royalist rector, Edmund Shallcross, was ejected from here by Henry Bradshaw.

Staircase House- Once the home of the Shallcross family, who also had a country manor house at Whaley Bridge. It was saved from demolition after a campaign by Stockport Heritage Trust and restored, is open to the public as part of the Market Place local history museum. It is a unique survival of a 15th-17th century merchant's home and warehouse. Reputed to be haunted by various ghosts.

Lancashire Bridge- The parapet was recently restored and the River Mersey opened up to view from the walkway above. The existence of a ford then bridge here led to the birth of the town. The battle of Stockport in 1644 was fought nearby because Prince Rupert wished to get his army across the river. He easily swept aside the local Parliamentarians who were outnumbered and withdrew.

Old Rectory- Now a restaurant and motel once the home of rectors and bishops of Stockport on Churchgate, it was originally timber framed a bit like Underbank Hall, the black and white townhouse of the Arderne family on Great Underbank. Rebuilt in red brick in the 18th century it was saved from dereliction and remodelled by Boddingtons in the 1990s. It has a blue plaque erected by Stockport Heritage Trust detailing its history. Cellars reputedly haunted.

Bramall Hall- Home of William Davenport whose tenants petitioned him to lead them in the defence of Manchester against cavaliers, but he refused. He was plundered of his horses and arms by both sides, even though he hid some horses with relatives at Woodford Old Hall. Bramall is open to the public as an outstanding Cheshire black and white mansion and former home of the Davenports, hereditary foresters of Macclesfield Forest. Reputed to be haunted by the Red Rider, harbinger of doom.

Poynton Pool- No stranger to violence (a police inspector murdered his wife and dumped her body here) it was also the scene of tragedy in the Civil War. Some Roundhead troopers from Stockport pulled lord of the manor, Edward Warren's pregnant wife, Margaret, from her favourite pony while she was out riding in the park and requisitioned it for the army. She went into premature labour and died a day after delivering twin boys April 1644. Later Edward built the Easter Sepulchre in St Mary's Church Stockport in her memory, which now confusingly contains the effigy of Richard de Vernon, priest.

Visit: **www.stockportheritagemagazine.co.uk for more publications and contact details**

The haunted terrace Marple Hall